Ultimate Cars

MUSTANG

A.T. McKenna
ABDO Publishing Company

visit us at
www.abdopub.com

Published by Abdo Publishing Company, 4940 Viking Drive, Edina, Minnesota 55435.
Copyright © 2000 by Abdo Consulting Group, Inc. International copyrights reserved in all countries. No part of this book may be reproduced in any form without written permission from the publisher.

Printed in the United States.

Library of Congress Cataloging-in-Publication Data

McKenna, A. T.
    Mustang / A. T. McKenna.
        p.   cm. -- (Ultimate cars)
    Includes index.
    Summary: Surveys the history of the Ford Mustang and its designs, engines, and performance.
    ISBN 1-57765-126-X
    1. Mustang automobile -- Juvenile literature. [1. Mustang automobile.] I. Title. II. Series.
TL215.M8M34 2000
629.222'2--dc21

                                      98-29328
                                        CIP
                                        AC

Contents

The Mustang

The Mustang is Ford Motor Company's most successful car. The first Mustang debuted on April 17, 1964. The four-seater was offered as both a coupe and a convertible model. In its first year, 418,812 Mustangs were sold. By March of 1966, the millionth Mustang came off the assembly line.

Some of the more famous Mustang models are the Shelby GT 350 and 500; Boss 302, 429, and 351; Mustang 2+2 Fastback; and the Mach 1.

A 1966 Mustang convertible

The Mustang was named by stylist John Najjar after the legendary P-51 Mustang fighter planes of World War II. Top speeds for these planes were 440 mph (708 km/h). While the Mustang is not that fast, it has been known to go up to 140 mph (225 km/h).

The Mustang is a sports car. A sports car is a car that is fast and has a sporty look. It is designed for the fun of driving. Sports cars usually have only two seats. Many times the word *sport* is used in the car's name.

A World War II P-5 Mustang

People Making Mustang History

Lee Iacocca seen here on February 10, 1998, at the age of 73.

There are many people at Ford Motor Company who helped build the Mustang. The "father of the Mustang" is Lee Iacocca. He was Ford's vice-president and division chief when the Mustang debuted. Henry Ford II was the head of Ford. He named Iacocca Ford's president on December 10, 1970.

Donald Frey was the product planning manager. He helped plan the

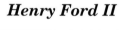
Henry Ford II

Mustang's production. He worked on things such as the costs involved and which new parts Ford needed to design.

Hal Sperlich was Frey's assistant. Sperlich was an engineer who was involved in building the first Mustang.

Eugene Bordinat was the director of styling. He created the Mustang prototype that was driven in the U.S. Grand Prix at Watkins Glen, New York, in 1962.

Semon E. "Bunkie" Knudsen was a longtime automotive executive at General Motors, Ford Motor Company, and White Motor Corp.

Joe Oros and Dave Ash were stylists, or designers. These two worked together to build a clay model body of the Mustang. Ford used Ash's design for the Mustang.

Semon E. "Bunkie" Knudsen became Ford's president in 1968. He put larger, more powerful engines in the Mustang.

Larry Shinoda was a designer. He previously worked on General Motor's Corvette. He came up with the name Boss Mustang for the 1969 model.

Creating a Car

It takes hundreds of people, from designers and engineers to mechanics to assembly line crews, to build a car.

The design department must come up with an idea of how the car should look. The designers usually draw several versions of the car before it is accepted. Then they make clay models of the design.

Designers use wood and foam to make a frame. This frame is the actual size of the car. Then, warm clay is laid over the frame and allowed to cool. This makes a life-sized model of the car. The model is then painted so it looks like the actual car.

The design of the car must be approved by the executives of the company. In the case of the Mustang, Henry Ford II was the final decision maker.

Once a car is approved, the engineers work with mechanics to build a prototype. A prototype is a very early version of the car. All the parts on the prototype are tested for strength and quality. The prototype is tested on a race track and on the street to see how it handles. The prototype is displayed at car shows to get people's opinions before the actual cars are produced.

After much research is done on the prototype, executives at the company decide whether or not to build the car. If the car is going to be built, changes are made based on the results of the testing and responses from people who saw it. Usually, the actual car does not look very much like the prototype.

Next, the car goes into mass production. This means that many cars are produced along an assembly line. An assembly line is a system used to produce many kinds of products, such as cars.

The six-passenger Ford Synergy 2010 prototype car is shown in 1995. The car is designed to use two power sources to get an economical 80 miles (129 km) per gallon.

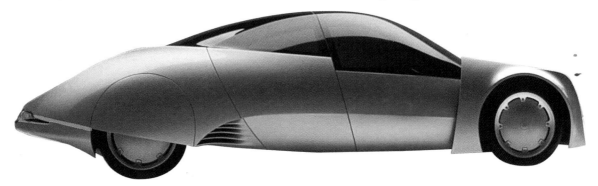

Each assembly line worker has a specific job to do. This man sands down the car.

Each worker on an assembly line has a specific job to do. The workers line up in rows and perform their jobs as the car moves down the line. One worker may put in the engine, while another installs the windows.

Ford planned to produce 75,000 Mustangs in the first year. Soon, Ford realized that it needed more assembly lines to keep up with the demand for the car. So, Ford converted two more plants to assemble the Mustang. More Mustangs came off the assembly line than any other car Ford had built!

A brand new mustang rolls off the assembly line.

The First Mustang

The Ford Mustang has an interesting beginning. A prototype for the first Mustang was raced in the U.S. Grand Prix at Watkins Glen, New York, in October, 1962.

But Lee Iacocca wanted a car that would appeal to more than race car drivers. So, it was back to the drawing board! Ford decided to build an all-new American sports car that was stylish, but affordable.

Ford wanted to introduce the car at the New York World's Fair in April of 1964. But, it was already the summer of 1962. So, a competition was held in Ford's design department. The top three designer teams were asked to create a clay model of a car in two weeks!

There were seven different entries in the car contest. The winner of the competition was Dave Ash, assistant to Joe Oros. His design was called the Cougar. He even placed a metal cougar on the grille of the car. The car was painted white with red wheels. Some of the executives didn't like the name. So, the car was renamed Mustang.

On March 9, 1964, the first Mustang rolled off the assembly line. Car dealerships had Mustangs in their showrooms on April 17, 1964. Ford made sure there was one Mustang for every Ford dealership in the country. The first Mustangs sold for $2,368. Both a convertible and a coupe version were offered.

The Mustang caused a huge sensation. Car dealerships were swamped with people wanting to get a look at this new and unique American car. People got into fights trying to buy the only one in stock. One dealer sold his model to the highest bidder. The man who bought it insisted on sleeping in the car overnight until his bank opened the next day so nobody else took it away from him!

The Mustang was a hot new car and everyone wanted one. By the end of the first year of production, Ford had sold 418,812 Mustangs.

The unveiling of the Ford Mustang at the 1964 World's Fair.

The Boss

Ford wanted to create a top car with a powerful engine to race on the Sports Car Club of America's (SCCA) Trans Am series and the National Association for Stock Car Auto Racing (NASCAR) series. The SCCA and NASCAR are sanctioning bodies for automobile racing. A sanctioning body is an organization which sets the rules for a type of racing, including how the cars are built.

Designer Larry Shinoda came up with the new name, Boss. The Boss 302 and 429 were Mustang models in 1969 and 1970. The Boss 351 was made in 1971.

The 1969 Boss 302 had one set of headlights inside the grille and another on the outside. It came in splashy colors, such as blue, orange, yellow, and white. It had a wide stripe along the side of the car's body and optional window slats. It also had front and rear spoilers. A spoiler is a piece added to the front or rear of the car that looks like a wing or fin. Spoilers direct air flow over the car to keep the front and rear of the car down when driving at fast speeds.

The 302 engine was rated at 290 horsepower at 5,800 rpm. Horsepower is the amount of power the engine has.

The initials *rpm* stand for revolutions per minute. This means that while the engine is running, it goes through the same sequence of events thousands of times per minute to keep the fuel flowing through.

The Boss 429 had a powerful V-8 engine. The number after *V* indicates the number of cylinders there are in the engine. Most modern passenger cars have four cylinders, V-4. The 429 engine rated 375 horsepower at 5,200 rpm. The 429 had a front spoiler and also a hood scoop. A hood scoop is an opening in the hood of the car that allows air in to help keep the engine cool. There were only 899 Boss 429s made, making it one the rarest of all Mustangs.

A 1971 Boss 351.

Mustang Timeline

The First Mustang

The Boss

Shelby Mustang

The Mach I

Mustang II

The Cobra

Fourth Generation

The Mach 1

The Mach 1 was a high-performance Mustang. It was a sporty car, meant for the race track or the road. It was called the "supercar for the masses." It was a very popular car, selling 72,458 in the first year.

The standard engine for the Mach 1 was the 351 two-barrel V-8 which rated 250 horsepower. There were two engine options with the Mach 1. They were the 320 horsepower 390 GT and the 335 horsepower 428 Cobra Jet.

The Mach 1 was known by its special body-side stripes and hood. The entire hood of the car was painted in anti-glare paint, the type race car drivers use. The hood air scoop was also painted black. The Mach 1 had optional hood pin latches. These are what racers use to make sure the hood stays down when racing at high speeds. The outside mirrors were painted the same color as the body.

Inside, there were high bucket seats and a sporty steering wheel. After the first year, the black paint was removed from the hood and stripes were added. The car also had different body-side stripes some years. But, it remained one of Mustang's most flashy models. The Mach 1 was built from 1969 through 1972.

Because of the elongated shape that Mustangs had during the years Bunkie Knudsen was in charge, some people called the front end of the Mach 1 the "Knudsen Nose" or the "Bunkie Beak."

Shelby Mustangs

Carroll Shelby was a famous race car driver. Shelby modified some of the Mustangs so they could be used for racing. He liked making production cars go faster.

Ford shipped partially completed Mustangs to Shelby's factory in Los Angeles. Shelby altered the appearance of the cars by removing all emblems and identification except for a small Mustang emblem on the front grille. Faster engines and high performance parts were installed in the cars.

The first Shelby Mustang was the Shelby GT 350 in 1965. It was built for the SCCA racing series. These were definitely race cars. There was no back seat! And there was no choice of color. All the early GT 350s were white with a black interior. They had bold stripes running from front to rear right over the top of the car. The GT 350 had a fiberglass hood with a scoop.

Top speed for this car was 140 mph (225 km/h) with a 306 horsepower Hi-Po 289 engine. The GT 350s won the SCCA's national championship from 1965 to 1967.

In 1967 the Shelby GT 500 was built. These cars had extra fiberglass added to the hood to create a long, pointed nose. There were air scoops on the sides. The cars no longer had stripes from front to back. Each of these cars had roll bars and shoulder harnesses for safety. A roll bar is a wide,

Carroll Shelby accepts a trophy after winning a race.

upside down, *U*-shaped bar that is padded with foam to protect the driver's head. If a car crashes and flips over, the weight of the car will be on the roll bar, not the driver. A shoulder harness is a special seat belt which keeps the driver from moving around while driving fast. Race car drivers use roll bars and safety harnesses in their cars.

Shelby Mustangs were the fastest and most powerful Mustangs ever built. Today, for those who collect old cars, the Shelbys are some of the most valuable Mustangs of all. Shelby Mustangs were made from 1965 to 1970.

Opposite page: The Shelby Cobra

Mustang II

Mustang sales had slowed down quite a bit. The sleek, slim car was now longer, wider, and heavier due to its larger engine. Iacocca knew that the people wanted a car like the original Mustang. So, he decided to design a new model that was smaller than the Boss and Mach 1.

Iacocca and Hal Sperlich flew to Italy to visit the Ghia car company studios for ideas. They met with Alejandro deTomaso. DeTomaso designed the prototype for the Mustang II. It came out in 1974, a time when there was a gas and oil shortage. The Mustang II was 6.6 inches (16.8 cm) shorter than the original Mustang. It had a standard V-4 engine, with a V-6 engine offered as an option. Top speed was just over 100 mph (160 km/h).

The Mustang II used the Ford Pinto's four-cylinder engine and various other Pinto parts to keep costs down. The Mustang II's economy made it a popular car during the mid-1970s gas shortage. It sold 368,000 in its first year. However, sales dropped in the following years, and in 1978, Iacocca was asked to leave Ford after 32 years. The last Mustang II was built in 1978.

The Mustang II was named Motor Trend *magazine's "Car of the Year" in 1974.*

Mustangs of the 1980's

The Mustang convertible was brought back in 1983, after a 10-year absence. The 5.0 liter, GT Mustang convertible cost $13,500. For the first time, it had a power roof, which meant the driver could put the top up and down with a button instead of by hand. And its rear window was glass instead of plastic. There were 23,438 convertibles sold that year.

In 1984, it was the twentieth anniversary of the Mustang. There were 150,000 Mustangs built. Ford put out a special anniversary model Mustang. It was white with a red interior. The twentieth Anniversary models had a badge on the dashboard with the owner's name engraved on it.

In both 1988 and 1989, production for the Mustang reached a record high of 200,000. The Mustang finally had new styling and a new interior. The cars had side skirts and a new rear spoiler. The 1989 model year was the Mustang's twenty-fifth anniversary.

Top speed for these new models was 150 mph (241 km/h). These new Mustangs were quieter, smoother, faster, and offered better handling than the older models.

*The 1984 twentieth anniversary Mustang
with an original 1964 model*

The Modern Mustang

The Mustangs of the 1990s were every bit as sporty and stylish as past models. In 1993, Ford released a special Mustang, the Cobra. The engine and other systems in the car were monitored by built-in computers. The Cobra had a 5.0 liter V-8 engine. There were 107 Cobra R versions made especially for SCCA racing.

Cobras are known for speed and style. Top speed for the 1995 Cobra R was 152 mph (245 km/h). These cars were designed to be raced. Anyone who bought a 1995 Mustang Cobra R had to be a member of a racing sanctioning body

The Multimatic Motorsport '99 Ford Mustang Cobra driven by the team of Scott Maxwell and Greg Wilkins makes its way around a hairpin turn at Sebring International Raceway, Friday, March 19, 1999, on the way to victory in the Motorola Cup three-hour race.

and have a valid race competitor's driver's license. These cars did not have a rear seat, radio, air conditioning, or power locks and windows. They did come with a special fiberglass hood.

In 1994, Ford released an all-new Mustang. This was called the Fourth Generation Mustang. The chassis and body had a completely new design. The hood was long and the sides had a sculptured look. The car had dual air bags and a tilt steering wheel. The back seat folded down for storage. The standard engine was a 145 horsepower V-6. The more powerful engine offered was a 215 horsepower V-8.

The Mustang is still a very popular car today. The "pony car" created great excitement when it was first introduced. And 33 years later, the Mustang is still going strong.

Glossary

Computer Aided Design (CAD) - computer software that allows a person to design a car by using a computer.

convertible - a car with a top that can be removed. Convertibles can have soft tops or hard tops.

coupe - a car with a permanent top.

debut - the first public appearance.

option - a piece of equipment or a feature on a car that is not included in the basic price. If a buyer wants to add a piece of optional equipment, he or she must pay the extra cost.

performance - the way in which a car handles.

V8 - a V-type engine has two rows of cylinders set at a 60-90 degree angle to one another, and a single crankshaft running through the point of the V. The number after the V indicates how many cylinders the engine has. V8s are V-type engines with eight cylinders. V-type engines may also have four (V4), six (V6), or twelve (V12) cylinders.

Internet Sites

Ford Mustang Homepage
http://www.fordheritage.com/mustang/
This is the official page of the Ford Mustang from the Ford Motor Company Web site. Click on the Mustang image to learn about the Mustang's history, build your own virtual Mustang, get information on Mustang's racing models, and see classic Mustang advertising art.

The Sports Car Club of America
http://www.scca.org
This is the official site of the Sports Car Club of America. Learn about the SCCA, scheduled racing events, and accredited racing schools. Get information on SCCA pro racing, and a road rally that everyone can compete in.

The National Association for Stock Car Racing
http://www.nascar.com
This is the official site of the National Association for Stock Car Racing. Learn about NASCAR, get technical tips from the Q & A page, and information and statistics on NASCAR tracks from coast to coast.

The Mustang Owners Club
http://www.mustang.org
This is the official site of the Mustang Owners Club. Get information on your local chapter, find Mustang car shows in your area, and see photos of the cover cars of *Mustang Times* magazine.

These sites are subject to change. Go to your favorite search engine and type in "Mustang" for more sites.

Index